Nig...

GIANT
CRAWLIES

The giant octopus began crawling towards me. The tip of one of its arms touched my hand and then it attached a sucker. It was soft and pliable. The octopus clambered up me, delicately touching every part of me with its tentacles as if it was a blind person feeling a new object. However, it certainly wasn't blind, because it squashed its huge eye up against my face mask. Was it peering in?

Nigel Marven's
GIANT CREEPY CRAWLIES

■ SCHOLASTIC

Scholastic Children's Books
Commonwealth House, 1-19 New Oxford Street
London WC1A 1NU

A division of Scholastic Ltd
London - New York - Toronto - Sydney - Auckland
Mexico City - New Delhi - Hong Kong

Published in the UK by Scholastic Ltd, 2000.

Text copyright ©, Nigel Marven, 2000

ISBN 0 439 99948 0

10 9 8 7 6 5 4 3 2 1

Printed by Cox & Wyman Ltd, England

The right of Nigel Marven to be identified as the author of this work has been asserted by
him in accordance with the Copyright, Design and Patents Act, 1988.

Contents

INTRODUCTION

I've always had a passion for creepy crawlies.
When I was a boy I wasn't interested in train sets
or racing cars, but I had an insatiable curiosity
about insects. My first ever pets were Indian
stick insects and I remember letting two of them
hang from each end of our washing line to see
which one reached the middle first. I was also
enthralled by the fact that tiny brown capsules
with neat yellow caps kept turning up in the
bottom of their cage. A few months later the
caps pushed off and spindly babies were walking
about on the privet leaves. But how was this
possible? All my stick insects were females —

didn't you need a male for that 'birds and the bees' business? In fact you don't, not in the weird world of insects. My pets were parthenogenetic, which meant they could produce babies that were clones of themselves without any other party being involved. As a teenager, I also delved into other corners of the invertebrate world, and kept scorpions, centipedes, woodlice and all sorts. Invertebrates – animals without backbones – make up ninety-seven per cent of the animal kingdom. There are 4,500 species of mammals, but between ten and twenty million species of invertebrates: we humans definitely exaggerate the importance of vertebrates – animals with backbones – because we are vertebrates ourselves.

But invertebrates are the most important life forms on earth; if they disappeared the rest of life would follow. Earthworms, for example, are vitally important all over the world. 'Nature's Ploughshare' was what the great naturalist Charles Darwin called them because of the way they churn the soil, letting the air get at it and bringing its minerals and nutrients near the surface so plants can flourish. Plants are also heavily dependent on insects to pollinate them, and, in fact, about a third of our diet is a result of insect pollination. Invertebrates are also a big help with some of the more unsavoury aspects of life on earth: without them to break it all down, for instance, we'd be up to our necks in dung!

Invertebrates can interact with us directly too. Thanks to the labours of silkworms (the caterpillar of a moth that feeds on mulberry) Britain's royalty can be married in the most wondrous silken clothes. Crabs, lobsters and prawns are all invertebrates, and they're some of the most sought after foods all over the world. But invertebrates can be our competitors too. They can destroy crops, stored foods and timber, and they can injure and kill our domestic livestock, sometimes even us.

I suppose we have a good excuse for ignoring invertebrates since most of them are tiny little things and we're huge. The wonderful excitement of seeing an earwig or lacewing fly in all their exquisite detail can disappear as we get older. Perhaps it's because as we get taller we grow up and away from the invertebrate world.

Grassland jungles, tangled flowerbeds and fallen logs can be almost at eye-level, when you're young. In my career making wildlife films, I've tried to compensate for that by spending much of my time crawling through undergrowth or lying flat on my stomach to get a creature's eye view of the world.

But not all invertebrates are tiny. On my travels I've discovered that there are some invertebrate species that are real life giants – they can be longer than I am tall, weigh as much as a dog or even fight battles with mighty sperm whales. I wanted to come face to face with these giant creepy crawlies and that is what this book is about.

Giant Earthworms

I was in Nantwich, Cheshire, about to witness one of the most eccentric sporting championships in the whole of England. The green grassy field was laid out in a series of small plots, three square metres each, their boundaries marked out with white tape. Each plot had a number and most had a garden fork embedded in the centre. Others had stranger contraptions: metal frames with plastic feet dangling close to the surface of the grass; corrugated washboards, shiny metal cheese–graters, and machines the like of which I'd never seen before, cobbled together from metal poles beaten into zigzags, a cricket bat and wickets, rubber tubes and even musical instruments, including a huge drum.

A throng of people were gathered around the edge of the field and there was anticipation hovering in the air. All faces were turned towards a bearded man resplendent in the blue and gold uniform of a town crier. He peered intently at his pocket-watch and began to count down. A hush descended on the assembled crowd. Then everyone looked towards the plots and became absolutely still. I could see their muscles tense as the town crier lifted his bell. Then he bellowed, "Let the Charming begin!" and dropped his arm.

As the bell peeled out there was a flurry and everyone sprinted towards their plots. Some people jumped on their garden forks and twanged them with sticks of metal or wood, while other people played their instruments close to the ground. Children jumped up and down. One woman in a cricketing outfit hit the grass with a bat, and ten plots away there was a man with a clown's make-up on, an orange wig, white trousers with red spots and huge plastic chicken-feet on which he bounced up and thudded down.

While everyone made vibrations into the ground in an attempt to draw its creatures to the surface, I ran between plots with the camera and sound man trying to film the action. We had to be on our toes because the World Worm-charming Championships, held in July each year, would only last for thirty minutes precisely. Remarkably, within seconds the pink heads of worms began to bob up to the surface. We joined in with a veteran competitor who told me 'premature worm grasping' could be a problem. You had to let them get far out enough from their holes before grabbing them – if you lunged too soon they'd withdraw and you could lose them.

Next we ran over to the judge to watch a disqualification: the chicken man had thrown soapy water on to his plot, and though worms wiggled in the suds this was clearly cheating since no chemical treatments are allowed. Two young girls were doing very well even though they squealed every time a worm pushed through the blades of grass. They wouldn't pick them up with their hands so they scooped up each wriggling prize with a wooden spoon. Another competitor pulled a string to make the plastic feet in his frame contraption (the device I'd seen earlier), jiggle about at the surface of the turf. He wasn't having too much success – perhaps the lightweight feet didn't pound the ground with enough force to bring out the worms.

This competition was a graphic illustration of why rooks and other birds gather on motorway verges, centimetres away from the cars hurtling past. The vibrations of the thundering vehicles have the same effect as twanging garden forks embedded in turf – they bring the worms up to the surface. I've also seen seagulls paddle the ground with their webbed feet, and this too brings worm snacks within range of their beaks.

All too soon the Nantwich town crier rang his bell to signal the end of the tournament, and now the serious job of counting the worms caught in each plot began.

The number of worms in a well-established garden or pasture can be phenomenal, perhaps as many as 25,000 worms per quarter–acre. They're important too. In fact Charles Darwin once wrote: "it may be doubted if there are any other animals which have played such an important part in the history of the world as these lowly organized creatures." In 1842 he spread broken chalk on a field of permanent pasture near his home and twenty-five years later (he was a patient man) he dug down to find the white chalk nodules twenty centimetres beneath the surface. They hadn't sunk but had been covered, at a rate of five millimetres a year, by soil material mined by worms from lower down. It's thanks to this hard work by worms that there aren't usually rocks or stones near the surface of lawns or flower borders and, what's more, the fine, rich soil brought up by worms is the perfect medium for plant growth.

Plants are also helped by the way worms keep the soil well drained – their burrows can be as deep as a metre beneath the surface. Worms provide these services as a by-product of tunnelling and feeding activities. They dig burrows by swallowing earth and feed at the same time, eating organic matter and microbes in the soil. The upper layers of earth are enriched with the fine soil that has passed through the worm's body; these deposits can be seen at the surface in the form of castings. Some of the larger kinds of worm also come to the surface to feed, dragging food such as leaves into their burrows. If you go out at night with a not-too-bright torch, you can see these activities going on, especially if it has just rained. You must tread carefully though, because vibrations on the surface have the opposite effect to vibrations sent underground and they cause the worms to shoot back to their tunnels. The dead vegetation that worms feed on is found everywhere so worms live in countless numbers all over the world. Their work is as valuable in tropical rain forests as in our suburban gardens.

At Nantwich their value is recognized by everyone and after the all-important count they're released back into the field. In the year we were filming, the winner caught 280 worms in the half-hour time limit. The world record, set in 1980, is 551 and that made it into the Guinness Book of Records!

The worm-charming championships were a fun introduction to these creatures but my search was for giant invertebrates. I wanted to see earthworms in other parts of the world that weigh up to 400 grams, average eighty centimetres in length and can be as thick as a garden hose. I simply had to meet them.

The film crew and I left winter behind in England and flew to Australia. The temperature change was radical: it was February and in the UK the temperature was near freezing, but it was high summer and 40°C in South Gippsland, a farming area three hours from Melbourne. Here in the dairy pastures scattered with eucalyptus trees we found the home of the Gippsland giant worm. These worms are found only in an area of about 100,000 hectares. On arrival we met researcher Beverley Van Praagh (a woman with a PhD in worms!) and the farmer, Bill Green. He took me out on his tractor to Beverley's excavation site and he told me some stories about the giant worm, who is something of a local celebrity. Bill was adamant that the worms on his land are the largest in the world, but as he's so proud of them he would say that! There are other contenders too, in South America and South Africa. There's a verified report of a South African species growing 2.6 metres long, and an unsubstantiated 'record' of a worm seven metres long. This type of worm has a slender body, however, and as the Gippsland Giant is much fatter, in terms of overall size, it probably takes the prize.

Bill told me his worms live in moist parts of the pasture. A few years before, he said, another farmer was herding some cows with his tractor and he heard strange noises coming from the ground. They were so loud he thought there was going to be an earthquake or something and he raced back to the farm for help. Bill chuckled because the other man, a local, should have known that this region's celebrity worms make loud gurgling noises. When they're moving about underground they can be heard even if they are two metres under. Apparently the sound is rather like water coming out of a bath. The more I heard, the more intrigued I became. I just hoped the ground was still wet enough to find the giant worms. Beverley had been wonderful because she had gone to great lengths to find me a worm. This was very difficult after the drought in the region that summer had dried out the ground.

I thanked Bill for the ride and jumped off the tractor. Beverley was meant to be at the edge of the pasture but when I went over I couldn't see her until I called, and then a head popped out from a hole in the ground. Because of the dry summer she and her assistant had had to dig a really deep hole to have any chance of locating the worm. The worms can dive down to four metres and the hole was half that. They had promising news, though.

In the palm of her hand Beverley held an amber–coloured case about eight centimetres long and shaped like a cocktail sausage. It looked and felt as though it was made of plastic, but in fact it was the egg capsule of the Gippsland Giant. I held the translucent case up to the light and could see a single embryo wriggling inside. My pulse quickened: even the unhatched baby worm was longer than any worm I'd seen in Britain. Beverley told me the eggs can take up to twelve months to hatch and the new born babies will take five years to reach maturity. Nobody knows how long a Gippsland Giant lives, but it could easily be a quarter of a century or more.

I jumped into the excavation with Beverley and watched in silence as her assistant carefully used the spade to slice into another layer of soil. Then there was a gurgle from the bottom of the pit just below where the spade had reached. I carefully prised the soil away with a trowel and a huge purple head reared up towards us before disappearing into a tunnel. Quickly but carefully, like surgeons performing an operation (the worms are easily injured), we followed the tunnel, almost removing the soil particle by particle. The burrow could go upwards, downwards, sideways or even double back on itself and we didn't want to cut the worm with our trowels. This was a delicate job, but after thirty minutes of meticulous labour, the whole of the worm's body could be seen and Beverley said I could lift the creature out.

This was thrilling and the camera crew filmed as I lifted up a Gippsland Giant in triumph. It had all the features of the earthworm back in my garden at home except it was an enormous ninety centimetres long – half my height! Its head was purple and pointed and the rest of it was a pinkish-grey colour. Its body was divided into segments, about 400 in all. I ran my finger along its body from the back towards the front. I'd never stroked an earthworm before, but now I could feel four pairs of bristles on each segment. These are important for the movement of the earthworm. Each of the segments is a fluid–filled compartment. Worms have this liquid skeleton to give them great flexibility when burrowing and crawling.

I could feel the power of this hydraulic system as the earthworm pushed through my fingers. In a tunnel the bristles would anchor the back end as a ring of muscles contracts at the front. The fluid-filled body segments can't be compressed so the front part of the body becomes longer and surges forward. The bristles are then used as anchors at the front end while those at the back are released, then muscle contractions bring the back end forward. By repeating this cycle the earthworm progresses through its burrow. This muscle arrangement is so powerful a contracted worm can be half the length of a relaxed one.

The giant had a big, fleshy saddle towards the front of its body. If you look at any mature worm in your garden you'll see the same thing. Earthworms are hermaphrodite, which means they are male and female at the same time, although two are needed to breed. The Gippsland Giant doesn't normally come to the surface, so the courting worms meet in a tunnel. They get close together with their heads pointing in opposite directions and a corset of mucus holds them closely aligned. They then pass sperm to each other, which is stored in special sacks. After they've parted, the saddles produce a detachable collar for the fertilized egg. The worm wriggles through this and the egg is passed into the collar, which is left behind. When it hardens it becomes an amber egg case just like the one Beverley had shown me earlier.

The Gippsland Giant is quite rare so we wanted to get it back into its tunnel as quickly as possible. No earthworms have eyes but their bodies are sensitive to touch or chemicals. I gently fed the purple head back into the dark tunnel, and slowly the worm hauled itself back inside.

I couldn't stop myself from smiling. I'd had a memorable encounter with one of the largest creepy crawlies on the planet and I couldn't help thinking what fun it would be if a Gippsland Giant turned up in the midst of the World Worm-charming Championships in Nantwich, Cheshire!

Worms – Fact Box

● Earthworms have four pairs of glassy bristles on every segment to prevent them from slipping.

● Giant worms in Australia can be heard on the surface, even if they're tunnelling two metres underground. The noise they make is like water running out of a bath.

● Earthworms spend most of their lives eating dirt.

● It's an old wives' tale that a worm cut in half grows into two new worms. That sort of serious injury would kill most worms but they can regenerate their hind ends if not too much is removed.

Robber Crabs

My next destination was a tiny speck of land in the deep waters of the Indian Ocean. After a four-hour flight from Perth, Western Australia, I could see the island below. It was, in fact, the peak of an undersea mountain. Rising 5,000 metres from the seabed, only the top 350 metres protrudes above sea level. The island was named by Captain William Raynors, who sighted it on Christmas Day in 1643 and decided to call it Christmas Island. I closed my eyes and thought of the great creatures that were hidden in that rainforest: crabs that can grow to the size of a dog – the biggest invertebrates to be found on land. I'd never seen a live robber crab and to do so is any naturalist's dream.

Noel, a ranger from the Australian Natural Park Service, was there to meet us and we soon loaded our twenty-five heavy cases of film and sound equipment into the waiting jeeps. Noel warned us to drive carefully; the roads were straight and level but a layer of clay meant they were slippery and treacherous when wet and we didn't want to skid off into the jungle.

Before taking us to the house where we were going to stay, Noel gave us a guided tour of the island. There's only one settlement so no special name is necessary – it's simply called 'The Settlement'! That's where we'd go for our meals. There's even an open-air cinema which shows a film once a week. The evening before had been movie-night, and we'd be gone before the next one – we only had four days to get our filming done.

To give a flavour of the island's natural history, we hoped to film some other species, as well as the robber crabs. We took some excellent footage of frigate and bosun birds. This was fantastic, but I couldn't wait to meet the hard-shelled giants.

The following day I awoke to see a cool mist hanging over the jungle. This wasn't surprising as the hot sun warmed the sopping landscape. Our visit was in March, towards the end of the rainy season which lasts from December to April. During this period the islands can be swamped with up to 200 centimetres of rain. This moisture, combined with tropical warmth, makes plants grow crazily and in this incredible lushness, animal activity becomes frenetic. That's why we'd come now and not in the dry season when many animals have to stay hidden in their burrows to avoid drying out.

Noel showed me a picture of an Arenga Palm. We needed to find one of these skinny trees with clusters of red berries; green wouldn't do because unripe fruits aren't sweet enough to attract the robber crabs. We spent a frustrating day finding many palms of the right variety but none with fruits at the right stage. The camera crew had now finished filming the frigate birds and were now really keen to film the robber crabs. Noel thought that without Arenga fruits, sausages could be the solution to our problem!

This sounded difficult to believe but I trusted Noel's judgement. So we set off with the gear on our backs which now included the necessary sausages and slogged through ankle-deep mud and tough-leafed vegetation towards a remote area called Dolly's Beach where Noel said we had a good chance of seeing the robber crabs. The going was tough and at times we could only make progress if Noel cut a path with his machete.

As well as robber crabs, Christmas Island has about twenty other species of land crabs. On our trek we could see that some parts of the forest floor looked as if they'd been swept clean of dead leaves, twigs and even seedlings. A closer look showed bright red discs that moved: red crabs are astonishingly abundant here – their population is about 100 million. I watched them carrying leaves into their burrows; they're the reason the forest floor is so clean. It must be a spectacular sight at the start of the rainy season when they migrate en masse to the sea to lay their eggs. Whenever we sloshed through a spring or stream there were other crabs. This time they were blue and – you've guessed it – they were called blue crabs, a species that needs to be near fresh water if it is to survive.

Sweating and muddy, we at last reached Dolly's Beach, a crescent of white sand enclosed by a coral reef just offshore. We made a fire, perched a battered frying pan on top and soon smoke from the sizzling sausages wafted into the jungle. Would robber crabs find this smell irresistible, as Noel had predicted?

A mere ten minutes had passed before two crabs trundled into view. These giants didn't disappoint: they were enormous and their colours were dazzling. One was blue with orange spots, while the other was mainly orange. I lay down on my stomach between them and the frying pan for a closer, crab's-eye view. They were quite nervous and backed away if I moved, but if I lay still they came really close. Both had scarlet eyes on stalks and two different sized pairs of antennae. These antennae are the sites of two of their most important senses: smell and touch. The smaller pair carry smell detectors which they use for detecting food at long distances, sniffing out fruit, dead animals, coconuts and even sausages! The longer antennae are sensitive to touch and they're used for manoeuvring in tight situations.

Both crabs had powerful claws but the left pincer was bigger than the right one. This is always the case and is a clue to the crab's ancestry. They're related to hermit crabs, the ones who live in borrowed snail shells and use their heavy and powerful left pincers as a door to close off the opening of the shell. (Check that out next time you find a hermit crab on the beach). I could even see that the robbers had a lobster-like tail tucked underneath their bodies – that's the bit that their hermit crab ancestors would have tucked into a shell.

If more proof was needed that these giant crabs originated from hermit crabs you just need to look at the juvenile ones. Like red crabs, the robbers go to the sea to spawn. Once the eggs hatch, the larvae spend some time floating about in the ocean. That's how the crabs colonized Christmas Island, by being washed here as larvae on ocean currents. The larvae transform into tiny crabs that spend the early part of their lives in the shallows and on damp beaches protecting themselves with a borrowed snail shell, just like their close relatives, hermit crabs.

One of the adult robber crabs that was close to me now showed how they earned their name, by stealing the barbecue tongs we'd used to turn the sausages! I crawled after it and pulled them from its pincers; they were Noel's favourite tongs, and you know how important barbecues are to Australians! Robber crabs are renowned for carrying away anything they can get their pincers on, and one was once even found dragging a whisky bottle into the bush!

Next the other crab showed how they earned their other name, coconut crabs. Realizing the sausages weren't in its reach, it turned to one of the coconuts that littered the beach and delicately put its pincers into a hole before tearing away some of the flesh inside. These crabs have a great fondness for coconuts and commonly shin up tall palms that sometimes tower twenty metres into the sky to cut off ripe nuts. Their pincers are certainly powerful but scientists still aren't sure whether they can break into this tough food themselves or whether they must rely on the nut cracking when it falls to the ground.

The crabs are scavengers too and won't turn down the putrefying flesh of a dead animal. Given the chance, they'll even hunt. One of the shop-owners in the Settlement told me about a huge crab that discovered a litter of kittens, and, despite the mother cat's desperate protests, trundled forward and dragged away the struggling kittens one by one.

Dolly's Beach had provided us with robber crabs, but only two; for a really spectacular film sequence we needed me to be surrounded by them. I was starting to worry because the next day was our last day on the island and even though we'd asked everyone we met to report to us if they came across a fruiting Arenga Palm, nobody had. As we packed our gear and struggled back up the muddy slope, I had a heavy heart – and even heavier legs on the long walk back.

About 100 metres from the jeeps I heard a

rustling sound. Peeking over a chest-height Pandanus Palm I saw a robber crab, then another, then another and another. I whooped with joy and called the others: it was the gathering we had been waiting for. There were at least twenty crabs beneath an Arenga Palm, all delicately tapping the ground with their legs and antennae. There were no fruits yet, but Noel thought the crabs sensed they'd ripen soon and they were testing the ground with their legs and feelers.

Unfortunately we couldn't film that day because the sun was too low in the sky to penetrate the thick forest, but we decided to return early the next morning. It was hard to sleep that night. Would the crabs be there tomorrow? Would we be disappointed? The next morning as soon as we arrived, I jogged over to the site to find out. The anticipation was unbearable! But the crabs were still there, and at last we would be able to film the sequence we'd travelled so far to achieve. Camera and sound were rolling as I crouched down amongst the crabs. As I came close, some of them seemed to be waving at me, brandishing either the left or right of the front pair of legs, depending upon which side I was approaching from. Rapidly snapping out a leg towards me wasn't in fact a greeting, it was a warning to potential predators to keep away. However, the shots we achieved were really funny: if I lifted my arm up and disturbed a crab, it lifted one of its arms as if it was copying me!

Christmas Island was probably the only place in the world where we could have filmed all this during the day. On the other tropical islands where they are found, robber crabs are nocturnal and only come out at night.

People have forced them to hide during the day because they're hunted for their oily flesh, which is a delicacy. Some of the crabs I was amongst now had a thirty-centimetre leg-span and they would amply feed six people. I was sad that these creatures are becoming rarer because of hunting. Lying down amongst them they looked so handsome with their hard outer coverings marked with red, blue, orange and even purple. They're the largest invertebrates on land and those beautiful hard suits are the reason why they, or any other land invertebrate, can't get any bigger. Our skeleton is on the inside, surrounded by soft tissue, but crabs and other creepy crawlies have a hard 'exoskeleton' – that's on the outside like a suit of armour – to which their muscles are attached. This suit can't expand as the crab grows, so to increase in size they have to moult their shells. The fresh new shell takes a little while to harden. If a land creepy crawly was any larger than the largest robber crab, the forces of gravity working on the newly moulted soft animal would make it collapse on itself before the shell could harden.

I was elated we had the film sequence in the can. My meeting with robber crab was a truly special experience, I'd met the largest land crab, an undisputed giant creepy crawly in terms of strength and size.

Robber Crabs – Fact Box

● Robber crabs are so well adapted for living on land that they would drown if held underwater.

● A robber crab drinks by picking up water droplets in its claws and putting them to its mouth.

● The world's largest population of robber crabs can be found on Christmas Island. Elsewhere on islands in the Pacific and Indian Ocean they've been hunted for their oily flesh which is a delicacy.

● Robber crabs scavenge on dead giant tortoises on Aldabra Island in the Seychelles and prey on tortoise eggs and hatchlings.

● The powerful pincer claws of robber crabs can tear metal like tinfoil and even bend a screwdriver.

● The world's largest crab is the Japanese spider crab, with a leg-span of two metres. It lives in deep water and never surfaces.

Giant Insects

I was looking for a bright green creature the size of a sausage in the sopping rainforest of Queensland, Australia. Cane toads jumped ahead of me wherever I walked. They'd been introduced from South America to control insects in the sugar-cane fields, but without predators their population had exploded and now they're a major pest.

A glistening vine ahead of me looked out of the ordinary and, as I got closer it retracted, drawing itself nearer to the branch it was hanging from. It swayed slowly in mid-air: an amethystine python about three metres long. It hung down, anchored to a branch above with its prehensile tail, patiently waiting for a small mammal or bird to come within range of its lightning-fast strike. Then, once its teeth were embedded in the prey's flesh, it would throw one or two coils around it, squeezing tighter and tighter until the prey suffocated. No pythons have venom; they kill by muscle power alone. I shone my torch along the snake's muscular body. It was marked with black diamonds on a brown background. If the light was right, its scales shone like an amethyst with a purple iridescence – which is how the snake got its name.

For the third time that evening there was a thundering sound above and, after a few seconds' delay, the rain battered its way through the thick canopy of leaves and I was soaked. Huge drops of water fell from the end of my nose. The leaves all around me had special pointed ends called drip tips, a special adaptation of rainforest trees to let the water run off after frequently being in the pelting rain.

I blinked water out of my eyes and there it was – the very creature I was seeking, hanging at head height on a real vine – not a python that looked like one! This was the Hercules caterpillar, the caterpillar of the world's biggest moth and maybe the biggest flying insect. It was using the vine as a scaffold, leaning out to feed on the leaves of the Bleeding Heart shrub which the vine lay against. I'd never really paid much attention to caterpillars before, but when they are this big you really take notice!

The caterpillar was more than fifteen centimetres long. Light blue in colour, each of its segments had four pale fleshy horns on the back. There was a vivid red spot in the middle of each segment on both sides of the body. These were the external openings to the caterpillar's breathing system. All insects have these holes (called spiracles) which lead into a series of breathing tubes. Insects don't have lungs like we do and oxygen passes via these tubes from the outside to the insect's tissues, and carbon dioxide passes out in the opposite direction.

Not that it looked as though this caterpillar needed to breathe much because it certainly wasn't over-exerting itself. The main muscles the

Hercules caterpillar exercises are those working its jaws; feeding and growing are really its sole purpose in life! As I watched, this one delicately drew another leaf close to its mouth. To do this it used the six pairs – I counted each one – of true legs right at the front of its body. All adult insects have six legs, but some larval stages (maggots, for example) have none, while caterpillars seem to have more than their fair share. Towards the back of the giant caterpillar there were five pairs of false legs or 'claspers'. It was using the fleshy soles of these to attach itself to the vine it was resting on. All this was a revelation to me. I'd seen many caterpillars before, but hadn't really appreciated them properly. All the features I've described can, in fact, be found on most caterpillars, but you have to look closely. Gently I collected the caterpillar. He didn't know it but tomorrow he'd be a TV star!

As I was filmed talking about the green giant I mentioned that it would soon undergo one of the most magical transformations in nature. This big, fat, sluggish leaf-eater would one day change into an elegant flying machine. As soon as it was a full-grown caterpillar it would produce silk from its mouthparts and spin a silken cocoon between two leaves. Inside that, most of its body would break down into a soup to provide the materials and energy for building the adult moth. A tiny cluster of cells provide the blueprint for the adult. They remain dormant in the caterpillar stage, until activated by the changing process or 'metamorphosis'.

This was easy to talk about but I didn't want to miss actually seeing this change in the flesh. So we collected ten Hercules caterpillars and transported them back to Britain. There are no rainforest plants in Britain except in botanical gardens, of course, but the Hercules caterpillar's gargantuan appetite could luckily be sated by privet leaves. Eventually the caterpillars would spin their cocoons; now, all we could do was wait. After two months, one moth emerged, then another. Surely some of the other eight would crack open soon. We hung the cocoons in a room next to my office in Bristol. It was as humid as a rainforest in there because we sprayed the room as well as heated it to give the optimum conditions for moth emergence. Volunteers took shifts at watching our cocoons night and day; a camera and tripod were in the room, set up to film, and the volunteers would telephone the cameraman as soon as they noticed anything happening.

Frustratingly, after two weeks of continuous observation, nothing happened. We waited some more, until finally we had a hatching, but it was the wrong sex. We wanted to film a female Hercules moth expanding her wings, not a male which is smaller. There's no way to be certain by looking at the cocoons what gender is inside them. Over the next two weeks four more cocoons hatched, but they were all males. Another began to smell: it had died early in its development. We could feel the other two wriggling but after a month our time had run out and the film was being edited. It turned out that they were females! They hatched just too late, after the documentary was finished.

I did manage to be filmed with an adult Hercules moth but she was an old lady of three days that had hatched deep in the rainforest without anyone watching. I say old because Hercules moths don't have any mouthparts, so they're unable to eat. They only live for about four days, which is as long as the fat deposits passed on from the caterpillar last. The caterpillar's job is to feed, but the moth's job is to breed: after mating the female will lay about 100 eggs before dying.

I let the moth take off from my face. She was a splendid insect, a rich brown in colour with a white line running down each wing. Each wing also had a tear-shaped white mark near the centre. This mark encloses a transparent window, but nobody's quite sure what this is for. It may help camouflage the moths by letting the background show through the wings.

Of course it was her size that was most impressive. Her wingspan was twenty-five centimetres. In 1948 there was a sighting in Queensland, just near where we filmed more than fifty years later, of a Hercules with a wingspan of thirty-six centimetres. Unfortunately, the report wasn't confirmed. If it had been, the

Hercules moth would be a match for the Queen Alexandra's birdwing of Papua New Guinea, the insect wingspan record-holder.

To enable them to fly, the moths are lightweights. Other than a tickling sensation from her feet, I could hardly feel the Hercules on my face. Her wings made a delicious breeze with their downdraft as she took off and fluttered away.

★ ★ ★ ★ ★

Now I turned my attention to the heaviest insects in the world. The first one wasn't that far away. It is found in the drier eucalyptus woodland on the rainforest edge in Queensland, Australia. Like the Hercules moth, it's nocturnal, so the film crew and I were on night shift once again.

These creepy crawlies are from a group of insects hated by most people, but really only a handful of species are a nuisance. They're the pests that have followed us around the world to invade our warm homes and hotels, the insects that scuttle across the floor or up walls like lightning when we switch on the light at night. These pests give all cockroaches a bad name; but for every species that's a nuisance, there are hundreds more that aren't. Most of the 800 species of cockroach are harmless forest-dwellers like the one we'd come to find, although our cockroach was particularly special, being thirty times the size of the typical cockroach and weighing thirty-five grams – as much as two sparrows!

I swept the beam of my flashlight over the ground and there, at the edge of its burrow, was a rhinoceros cockroach. I pointed to its position and whispered to the crew that I was going to dive on it. I heard the camera whirr and fell forwards. I just about managed to clutch the creature but nearly dropped it because of a sharp pain in the palm of my hand. This cockroach has powerful spiny legs for tunnelling and it was kicking me with these. I quickly changed my grip so I held it at the side of its body and now its legs were harmlessly flailing against air.

He soon calmed down. I could tell his sex because the dorsal shield on the front of his body had a deep indentation whereas females have a flat shield. He was so handsome, with his armour plating as brown and shiny as a fresh conker. I held him vertically to show the camera his head, and peering at him in that position I was sure cockroaches must have been the inspiration for the Darth Vadar character in *Star Wars*. Once all the close-ups were finished I gently released him. The dry eucalyptus leaves that are the main food for rhinoceros cockroaches crackled as he scurried over them.

He'd felt quite weighty in my hands, but I knew that there are even heavier insects to meet. The creature I really wanted to see is one of New Zealand's oldest residents: the weta, a giant flightless grasshopper. I can't resist odd animals and this one had to be bizarre because the native Maoris call it the 'ugly thing'. On top of that, it's the prey of the tuatara – a reptile I've dreamt about seeing since I was old enough to read.

The approach to their island home was really exciting. The helicopter skimmed the top of dark grey cliffs that plunged into the ocean 250 metres below. Once we'd landed in a small clearing, the pilot left the engines running and the rotors turning as we unloaded our gear. Then he was up and away, saying he'd be back to pick us up in three days. We'd landed on one of the Poor Knights Islands in the Pacific Ocean off New Zealand's North Island. The top of the island was cloaked with weird trees, twisted and gnarled into extraordinary shapes and the strange calls of bell birds echoed around this fairy-tale forest. I felt I was in a lost world, and to some extent I was. The New Zealand group of islands was separated from the continents eighty million years ago. That was in the latter part of the age of the dinosaurs. Land mammals and snakes never made it to New Zealand. They missed the boat, as it were! We soon set up our camp site, but I would have to wait a bit longer for the creatures I was so excited about seeing. They're nocturnal, so another night shift lay ahead of us.

During the day I snoozed in the tent, and my alarm call at dusk consisted of the cackles and coos of sea birds. I looked out of my tent and there the birds were: Buller's shearwaters, looking completely out of place in a dense forest. They had soft grey backs, white bellies and black markings on their faces. They ran and jumped on the forest floor, scooting about erratically as they pushed off with their webbed feet. I followed one and watched as it disappeared underground, where the racket continued. In fact the bird was at the end of its burrow gossiping with its mate, who was being relieved of the task of incubating eggs. After they had cackled to each other for a while, the departing bird would head back out through the forest and launch itself into the air from a boulder or cliff, heading out to sea to feed. The bird that was left behind would have to incubate the eggs all night and all the next day before it could feed again.

My mind returned to the creature I'd wanted to see most – the tuatara. It's the top predator here, a reptile, supplementing its insect diet with sea-bird eggs and chicks. After an hour of looking I heard a rustling in the leaves. I checked with Richard Parrish, our adviser from the New Zealand Department of Conservation;

I meet a real-life worm charmer.

A robber crab – claws and all!

A giant squid – a beautiful creature!

A giant cockroach – about as close as you can get!

The Australian burrowing cockroaches
make quite a handful.

I'd never seen such a large and beautiful caterpillar.

A giant ant – one of nature's great survivors.

The Hercules moth in all its glory.

A lifetime's ambition fulfilled – I meet a tuatara.

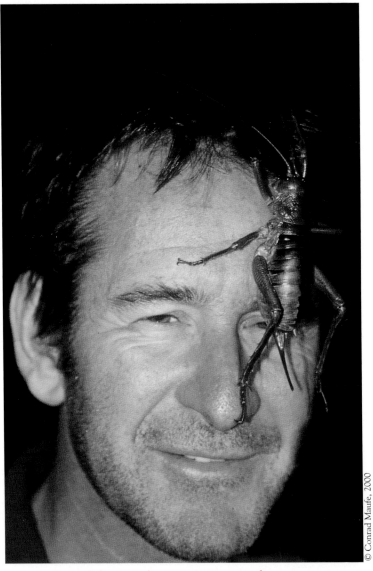

A real face-to-face encounter with a weta.

tuataras are rare and I wanted his permission to hold it. He told me how to grab it gently and firmly, but to be careful of its bite – if it bit me the serrated jaw bones could draw blood and the reptile could hang on for half an hour or more! The tuataras' lack of proper teeth is one of the main features that distinguishes them from lizards, and they're the one surviving member of a reptile group called the Rhynchocephalians or 'beak heads'. The tuatara is the only reptilian survivor from the age of dinosaurs. All its ancestors died out 135 million years ago.

Slowly, I moved my hand closer. The tuatara was as still as a statue. I grasped it just behind the head as Richard had told me to and carefully cradled it in my arms. What a magnificent creature it was.

The most striking feature of the tuatara is a crest of soft white spines on the top of its head and down its back. Tuatara is a Maori word meaning 'lines of spears' and that's exactly what the white scales look like. The tuatara's eye is beautiful, a deep brown with flecks of gold and a vertical pupil like a cat's. A lifelong ambition of mine had been realized. I had finally seen a tuatara in its natural habitat. We finished filming the ancient reptile and I reluctantly let it go. It disappeared into the forest. Wow! It truly was an amazing experience. As we finished up for the day I said, "Now we've found the predator, we still need to find its prey, an insect of enormous proportions."

The following evening we set off in search of a giant weta, a type of grasshopper. The best chance of finding one of these incredible insects was to shine our flashlights along tree trunks and boughs in the darkness. Perhaps because they're in danger from tuataras on the ground, giant wetas stay perched above it for much of the time. They're another ancient group with a lineage as old as the tuataras'. Fossilized wetas have been found in rocks that are 180 million years old. There are ten giant species, and the largest beat most of the world's biggest insects in terms of weight and bulk: these insects are bigger than house mice.

Because there are no native land mammals in New Zealand, wetas have evolved to behave like mice, emerging from daytime shelters to feed on greenery and seeds after dark. Of course, this lack of mammals soon changed when man reached New Zealand a mere one thousand years ago. Man brought his followers with him including mice, rats, cats and foxes. New Zealand's birds and insects couldn't cope with the invasion. Because of the lack of native predators many of them had become flightless and they couldn't escape the new hunters. In this way, the population of great wetas was decimated and they now mainly survive on small islands that have escaped the invasion of rats and mice. The Poor Knight's Islands are one such oasis, free of alien animals, and that's why giant wetas are still quite common there.

On a branch some three metres up we saw our first giant weta. It looked frightening and bristled with long legs armed with spines and huge antennae. Richard needed to weigh it for his scientific work so I offered to catch it. Luckily the tree was easy to climb and I hoisted myself up quickly. Putting my hand around my prize, I jumped back down and carefully put the weta in the polythene bag Richard was holding. He hung the bag and the weta from some scales – fifty-five grams: this was a pretty big individual. I lifted her out again so the film crew could film me handling her. I could feel it was a female because at the end of her body there was a wicked-looking sabre-shaped appendage that looked as though it could have been a sting. In fact, it was the tube that female wetas use to probe into the ground to lay their eggs. I was relieved at how docile she was. She could have lashed out with her spiny legs or even bitten me with her mouth parts, which are tough enough to cut through leathery leaves, but instead she crawled over my hand before picking up speed and running up my shirt, over my shoulder and down my back to the ground. She scored very high on the fearsome looks scale but zero for aggressive behaviour!

The next two days were idyllic. For once we didn't have that will-we-won't-we feeling about finding the animals we were trying to film. We could concentrate on getting exquisite close-ups of the wetas, tuataras and shearwaters. All too quickly, however, we were packing up once more and waiting next to that rock platform for the helicopter to pick us up. As we waited I thought about my job. My mum and dad thought I'd grow out of my passion for creepy crawlies and reptiles, but I never did and now I've made them my career. I'm so lucky to do what I love so much. When I first read about tuataras I never imagined I'd ever hold one, and as for the giant weta I felt privileged to be one of the very few people ever to be in the company of one of the most spectacular and unusual insects on earth.

Creepy Crawly – Fact Box

● Arthropods are animals with jointed legs covered with an external or exoskeleton. They include insects, centipedes, crabs, lobsters, spiders and scorpions.

● For every man, woman and child on earth, there are 200 million insects.

● There are three species of wetas, flightless grasshoppers, from New Zealand that have tusks. The males use these for fighting.

● Rhinoceros cockroaches are devoted mothers, protecting and feeding their babies in a burrow until they can fend for themselves.

● Africa's Goliath beetle is the biggest insect in the world. It's six centimetres across, fifteen centimetres long and weighs 100 grams.

Giant Squid

One-and-a-half kilometres down, in the deep cold waters between mainland Australia and Tasmania, it is pitch dark – there isn't a glimmer of daylight down here, ever! The only illumination comes from the sparks and flashes made by living creatures. Many fish, shrimps and molluscs have pockets of light-producing cells called photophores which glow in the dark. They use these lights to communicate with each other, for catching or attracting things to eat, even for frightening away things that could eat them!

Suddenly there is an explosion of brilliant green flashes like an underwater firework display.

A predatory fish, more than a metre long, has lunged through a shoal of smaller fish which switch on their lights in alarm. The flashes light up the jagged peak of undersea mountain that rises up from the sea floor another one-and-a-half kilometres below. The bursts of light distract the predatory fish, but it still manages to gobble up three of the smaller fish in quick succession.

Then, attracted by the explosions of light, a vast shape glides over the peak of the sea mountain. It has the largest eye of any living creature: the lens inside is as big as a golf ball and the whole structure as large as the hub cap on a car. The twelve-metre-long creature seems to hover like a spacecraft, but then it surges forward. Its torpedo-shaped body is built for speed and this allows it to pick up momentum quickly. This creature is rocket-propelled, pushing itself forwards by forcing water out of the back end of its body. Zooming forwards, it aims its two longest tentacles (it has ten in all) at the predatory fish which now has a fourth smaller fish wriggling in its jaws.

The long tentacles of the giant squid are tubes

of muscles. By contracting these muscles the creature shoots the tentacles forward, a process that's a bit like squeezing toothpaste from its tube really fast. The tentacles have suckers at the end and in another second the large fish is caught between them as they clamp down on its body like a pair of pliers. The force is so great that the bodies of the small fish it has already eaten are spat back out into the sea. The squid's feeding tentacles, which are thicker than a man's arms, now retract and the catch is pulled back to the rosette of arms around the squid's head and into its mouth, where the powerful parrot-like beak makes mincemeat of the food.

In fact, I was at the surface, between Australia and Tasmania, on a fishing trawler one-and-a-half kilometres above the place where this dramatic scene could have been happening. Nobody can be exactly sure about the details of how giant squid hunt because perhaps the single most fascinating thing about them is that no living specimen has ever been seen alive by anyone! The film crew and I were hoping that we might be able to film a dead or dying giant squid being hauled up in the nets. Nearly thirty of these creatures have been caught in New Zealand and Australian waters in the last couple of years.

Throughout history a few hundred giant squid have been accidentally caught in trawl nets or become stranded or beached, and that's how we know they exist. Their bodies have washed ashore in New Zealand, Newfoundland, Japan, South Africa, Norway, Iceland and Denmark. The earliest realistic record came from Iceland in 1639, but there could have been sightings before that and it's possible that it was such sightings that led to stories of the kraken, a many-armed sea-monster that could reach as high as the top of the main mast of sailing ships. When such creatures attacked they would apparently wrap their arms around the hull of a ship and capsize it. In Norway, in the twelfth century, the kraken was described as a floating island more than four kilometres across.

As we rocked and rolled in the ocean off Tasmania, I'd have been quite happy to be taken by a kraken! This was the first time in my life that I'd been sea sick and it was a terrible feeling.

I wanted a quick end to the waves of nausea, and as my cabin jerked violently before my eyes and sea water exploded against the portholes, it seemed to me that a kraken attack would at least have ended my misery.

All we managed on that four-day voyage of sickness was to film me next to the nets as they were hauled aboard, while I talked about Giant Squid tentacles. At the tips of the Giant Squid's tentacles are feeding-clubs which sometimes get ripped off and entangled in the nets. I explained how scientists think that the mass of trapped and frightened fish flash their lights and attract giant squid which then attack the nets. As the nets are dragged upwards to the shallow surface waters the giant struggles to free itself, and the tips of the feeding tentacles are torn off in the tussle.

At last the ship turned around and headed back to port. With the knowledge that I was only twelve hours from terra firma, I began to enjoy the voyage. Huge flocks of albatrosses – my favourite birds – skimmed the waves, tracking the trawler like gulls. Back on land, soon we were driving, not sailing, to a remote Australian beach so I could see for myself just how large a real giant squid is. Our giant squid had been washed up a few months before and the Tasmanian museum and art gallery in Hobart had kept it preserved in a freezer. They had agreed to use a fork lift truck to take the frozen corpse back to the water's edge so I could be filmed next to it using my body to give a sense of scale to the viewer.

After four hours of thawing – and a near disaster when the carcass was nearly washed out to sea – it was ready, and I had my first look at a real giant squid in the flesh. It certainly was a remarkable creature. The main part of the body, called the mantle, had a fin along its length to help with swimming. The front end, with its eight arms, but missing its two feeding tentacles, looked like a huge alien flower. Surprisingly, squid and octopus are molluscs, so they're actually related to snails and slugs. But they've evolved to be fast-moving hunters and are in a group of their own called cephalopods, which means 'head-footed'. I could see why when I gazed down at the rosette of arms at the front end of this giant squid. I'd heard that some fishermen had tried eating the bodies or body parts of giant squid that ended up in their nets, thinking they may be as tasty as calamari (smaller squid that do taste nice). They soon gave that up, however, and now I could find out why, first hand. I licked one of the arms which tasted awful, just like floor cleaner. In fact giant squid have pockets of the chemical ammonia, in their flesh, which they use to maintain the right buoyancy when they're gliding through their ocean realm. Next I parted the arms and opened the giant squid's mouth: there was a sharp horny beak. I wouldn't have done this with a live one – scientists think that they could snip off a finger with ease.

I looked at the giant's body one last time. The sun was setting and the museum workers had to get it back into the freezer as they hoped to display it later in the museum. It was sad to see that great creature reduced to a collapsing pile of anaemic-looking flesh, but I thought how brilliant it will be when a living giant squid is eventually captured on film or video. Many expeditions with deep-sea submersibles have tried, but so far there's been little success. Once a camera was even attached to a sperm whale, the only predator of the adult giant squid, but that didn't get a result either. Just imagine if someone manages to film a battle between a giant squid and a sperm whale! Many mysteries will be resolved. The whale only has teeth in its lower jaw, so how can it grab a fast-moving squid? Or does it? Some people think it emits a focused beam of sound to stun its prey. Anyway, these 'firsts' are what scientists and wildlife film-makers dream about. I'd certainly be at the front of the queue to watch that footage!

For now it's impossible for me or anyone else to see a living giant squid, but there's another sea monster that can be tracked down. Creepy crawlies can grow to be giants in the sea because unlike air, water provides support for their bodies. The biggest giant squid weighs a massive two tons, but there's also an eight-armed cephalopod which grows to a huge size – the giant octopus and that can be encountered by divers. To get to grips with this creature a film crew and I travelled to the waters around Vancouver, Canada.

I'd met a giant octopus before, when I was making a film about the marine life of Russia. This giant is found on both sides of the Pacific – they're all along the coast of Eastern Asia as far south as Japan and, on the American side, their range extends from California northwards to Alaska. Even though we'd already met, I was excited about another encounter, particularly as the waters of the Pacific North West are a world of giants.

We filmed some of the supporting cast on our first dive, when we went down to thirty-five metres and gradually worked our way up into shallower water. Our first creature, an irregularly-shaped white mass the size of a bus, looked more like a plant but, in fact, this strange structure was a group of cloud sponges. Sponges are animals that live like animated filters, straining out minute organisms contained in the stream of water that passes constantly through their bodies. Their soft bodies are supported by a skeletal framework of tiny slivers of silica. Some other sponges have a skeleton of a horny elastic substance called spongin, and the skeletons of these sponges are the ones we sometimes use for bathing (although nowadays most household sponges are made artificially). In cold water, cloud sponges grow slowly and can live for a very long time: the colony I smam past could well have been more than seven thousand years old!

At twenty metres, sticking out from some sandy gravel, were what appeared to be a group of black flowers nearly a metre high. But when my shadow passed over them, the 'petals' disappeared inside the stem. These weren't flowers at all but black feather duster worms. They manufacture their own glue to make a protective tube of small stones and sand and, when the coast is clear, they stick their feeding arms out of the end to trap any food particles in the currents flowing around them.

Next to the bed of worms there was a sausage-shaped object, nearly sixty centimetres long, lying on the sand. Another giant, this time a sea cucumber. Related to sea urchins and starfish, this creature has a surprise in store for any would-be predators. I found this out when I tried to pick it up: it immediately shot a sticky mass from the front of its body. It was literally throwing out its insides to deter me from eating it! This sounds drastic, but simple creatures like this can grow a new set soon enough.

I checked my dive gauge and realized I should return to the surface soon. Since we'd gone so deep, our time underwater was limited. I tapped the cameraman on the shoulder – he'd just finished filming me touching the sea cucumber – and pointed to the surface. He nodded in agreement – his air was running low too. We ascended slowly: we had to do this to avoid a build up of nitrogen in our muscles which could lead to the dreaded bends (an excruciating condition that results from bubbles of nitrogen in your blood). I watched our silver bubbles fly up past a jagged rock wall, where there was a small cave with a shelf outside. On that shelf there was a pile of empty crab shells and pincers. I tried not to smile too much – if I did, water would flood into my mask – but it was difficult not to. The pile of crab shells were the dinner leftovers from the creature we were looking for. I'd found the lair of a giant octopus.

We returned later when it was dark for a night dive. Even though the giant octopus can be out and about during the day, they're more likely to be active at night. It's always eerie diving at night and I gulped air through my regulator as we descended. My nerves made me suck in air and the noise of my breathing seemed to be magnified by the dark water. I couldn't help thinking about the sea monsters in *The Toilers of the Sea*, a novel written in 1866 by Victor Hugo, where there is an account of a fight between a man and an octopus whose leathery arms had suckers with sharp points that tore through human flesh. After the book's publication, debates about the dangers of the 'Devil Fish' raged in Paris, but I knew that there was no real threat from an octopus – unless you were a crab or a lobster of course!

I still had a niggling worry though. If we found an octopus I planned to be enveloped in its arms on film so that I could show the viewer its size. These animals average twenty kilograms in weight with an arm-span of five metres. The biggest, caught in Western Canada in 1957, was huge with a 9.6-metre arm-span. These creatures are strong and can be curious – they're thought to be as intelligent as a house cat. What if the octopus I was meeting became inquisitive about my regulator or air hose, grabbed them and cut off my air supply? It was unlikely, but I couldn't help thinking about it.

We shone our lights around at fifteen metres: a few fish shimmered in the beam of the light but there was nothing else. Then I pointed the beam upwards and suddenly there was a huge shape, broader at one end and tapered to a point at the other. It shot forwards with two spurts of movement and then the thin end came apart, revealing eight arms which flowed out to the sides and formed a wing shape. The giant octopus then glided gracefully down on to a flat platform of rock ten or fifteen metres away. It had moved in spurts because, like the giant squid, octopuses take water into their bag-like bodies and expel it through a siphon to jet-propel themselves forwards.

The cameraman filmed over my shoulder as I approached the octopus. Its body and arms combined were as long as me, and I'm 1.9 metres tall. I grabbed hold of a rock to anchor myself next to it, and the cameraman did the same – the current would have carried us away if we didn't have anything to hold on to. At first the octopus drew itself into a tight ball, but then it unfurled and began crawling towards me. The tip of one of its arms touched my hand and then it attached a sucker. It was soft and pliable, not spiked like the fictional creature in the Victor Hugo novel.

Slowly I got myself into a kneeling position. The octopus clambered over me, delicately touching every part of me with its arms as if it was a blind person feeling a new object. However, it certainly wasn't blind, because it squashed its huge eye up against my face mask. Was it peering in? After a minute or so of close investigation, it lost interest in me and scrambled over the rocks to disappear behind a curtain of seaweed flowing in the gentle current. This time I couldn't stop myself from smiling a lot and water flooded into my mask, so I tilted my head back and blew through my nose to clear it. When I could see again I noticed that the cameraman was clearing his mask too: he'd been smiling as broadly as I had – both of us were elated by this sequence of film. We'd shown that unless you provoke them, octopuses are gentle giants. Eight-legged malicious sea monsters are creatures of our imagination found only in novels or nightmares.

Squid and Octopus – Fact Box

● Squid, including giant ones, are the main prey of sperm whales. One whale was found with 28,000 squid beaks in its stomach.

● The giant squid has been responsible for many 'sea monster' stories, usually when dead or dying ones float next to ships.

● Squid eyes are remarkably like our eyes in their construction. The giant squid has the largest eye of any animal – the size of a dinner plate. It is larger than the eye of an elephant or whale.

● Nautiluses are related to squid and octopuses but they have an external shell. Squid have a reduced shell inside their bodies while octopuses have no shell at all.

● A giant octopus produces 80,000 rice grain sized eggs. She guards and cleans them without feeding until they hatch six months later, then she dies: the devoted mother dies of starvation.

Army Ants

Stretching towards the sky, a huge tree had fought its way upwards to pierce the dense canopy of the Amazon rainforest, so its leaves could have unrestricted access to sunlight. Fifty metres below, the base of this giant flared out into massive buttress roots. A dozen of these extended from the trunk to the ground. These roots provide extra support for the skyscraper of wood and leaves. One of the supports was decaying, though, and dark holes led up under the buttress where it met the main trunk.

Inside this cavern, a giant predator was resting; a predator that can be nearly a kilometre long and fifteen metres across, a carnivore so vicious that given the chance, any animals, whether they walk, hop, fly or run will get out of its path. I say 'given the chance' because this hunter can move at great speed and the slow or unwary don't stand any chance at all. I had never seen this predator before, but I wanted to, and that's why I slept uneasily inside a tent, only two metres away from the great tropical tree with the buttress roots. I was waiting for the predator to wake up. It was still dark when it did.

Earlier in the night, rain had pattered on my tent. The noise I heard now sounded the same, but no raindrops were falling. Turning on my flashlight, I could see a black shape gliding over the outer skin of my refuge. I felt for my glasses and the shape resolved into a shifting mass of thousands of long-legged marching insects: my tent was enveloped by swarming army ants. I dressed quickly and put on my boots, being careful to tuck my trousers into the tops of my socks. The army ant swarm was on the left-hand side of the tent, so I gingerly opened the front zipper and half jumped, half ran, from the right side, into the forest. Because of the dense canopy of leaves the jungle was still grey, even though the sun was straddling the horizon, so I still couldn't clearly see any details of the scurrying insects around me. On logs, with lighter bark, I could see the patterns the ants made as they marched in one direction, in long orderly columns, hence the name 'army ants'. Another regimental line was surging over a pile of light brown leaves.

From a distance, it seemed as if a black ribbon was gracefully undulating over the obstacle. I knelt down next to the column on the log. There was a small gap from this log to a nearby branch, but that had been bridged by living ants; they had interlocked the claws on their legs so their sisters could race over them from the log to the branch. Even though the light wasn't good enough to make out individuals, I knew they were sisters, because the workers in an ant colony are all female, originating from a single queen.

The queen never raids, she was back in the tree-hole being pampered, fed and cleaned by the workers; her sole purpose in life is to produce eggs. Much larger than the others, and very different in structure, her head and legs are attached to a body that from the outside looks nothing more than a white-and-brown bag. But inside it is crammed with everything necessary for an egg production line. The queen can produce up to 300,000 eggs in a three-week period, 2.5 million eggs in a year. The bigger her colony is, the more successful it is at hunting as a group. I could now make out what her offspring looked like, as at last the sunlight filtered through the mosaic of leaves and twigs above me.

The majority of the ants taking part in the procession looked pretty much the same: about a centimetre long with a brown head and light yellow abdomen. These were the medium workers. They do many jobs for the colony, from catching and cutting up prey, to building bridges using their own bodies, to regurgitating food for the larvae back in the colony. Looking closely, I could see others that were slightly larger in overall size, and size of jaws. They were sub-majors. We would see them in action later. Their main job is to bring back the victims of each hunt. Other workers were very obviously different. They were larger, and pale-coloured, with huge scissor-like jaws – these workers are called majors or soldiers. Their role was obvious: the defence of the colony and all its members. There is another caste of workers called minims, but they rarely leave the vicinity of the queen, spending all their time bustling around her and the eggs and larvae. All these different castes of workers, each with a different role, are needed for the successful operation of an ant colony.

The forest floor was splashed with sunlight now. As I'd been observing the ant column in front of me so closely, I hadn't noticed another column of ants swirling around my feet. From reading lots of jungle adventures when I was a boy, I'd never have believed that anyone could stand in the middle of an army ant swarm – surely they'd soon be charging up my legs and ripping my clothes to shreds before stripping my flesh to the bone – but of course these things only happen in fiction or Hollywood. I stood still so as not to disrupt the chemical trail which the ants lay down to find their way. If I did, they might swirl around in confusion, running in all directions, perhaps right up my body. Shaking my legs in panic would be wrong too, because then the ants would be disturbed and this could prompt an alarm chemical that would make the others attack me. I hadn't disturbed them too much and they didn't climb any farther up than my knees. These army ants can sting and bite, but they didn't do either. Even if I was unconscious or tied down, it's unlikely they'd try to eat such a large animal.

Their jaws are designed for clasping and dismembering smaller prey, not tearing away human flesh. There are reports of driver ants, the African cousins of these Amazon army ants, killing and feeding on tethered livestock. The jaw arrangement of driver ants is different from army ants so they can slice off slithers of mammalian flesh, but they wouldn't get the chance if the animal could run away.

Being eaten alive by ants is still a nasty thought. It took some churning calls, almost like the growls of miniature jungle cats, to bring me out of my reverie. I had company, but the calls were from birds, not cats. Their calls were a sign that the ants had begun to raid in earnest. The birds that were scolding me were ant birds, perhaps their call mimicked a carnivore's growl to frighten would-be ground predators like me. I stared intently into the gloom; at first I could only make out dark shapes flitting amongst the shadows, but then one of the birds perched in a pool of sunlight. It had a goggle-eyed look, because of a patch of bare red skin around its eyes. Otherwise, it was black with chestnut wings: it was a red-winged bare eye. I only had a few seconds to enjoy this striking robin-sized bird, before it flitted back into the shadows. Then another type of ant bird showed itself. This one had a smaller head, blue skin encircling its eye and a brown back. These two ant birds are what biologists call professional ant followers. This means that they pretty much depend on the insects and probably wouldn't be able to survive without them. About fifty species of bird regularly forage with ant swarms, but surprisingly none of them actually eat ants.

Now, as the ant swarm spread out into a broad, fan shape, I could see how the birds feed, for as the formation of army ants pressed forwards, the leaf-litter ahead of them began to move. It seethed with prey attempting to escape. Anything in the swarm's path broke cover, as the ants charged under logs and leaf litter, they even flushed out nocturnal creatures from their day time refuges. I saw crickets, spiders and even a scorpion trying to flee. Many were tirelessly run down, as the ants are much faster than most other invertebrates that they encounter. Once caught, the prey is overwhelmed by a sea of ants. It's as though the prey is caught in sticky, black treacle. Their limbs move in slow motion as they try to escape, but then sheer weight of numbers beats them, and they disappear under a seething mass of biting, stinging ants. Now the prey is dismembered, the ants nip off portions of legs and antennae wherever there is a joint or other point of weakness. Even small snakes and lizards can be overcome and cut up in this way.

Ant birds were watching the action as

intently as I was. Any insects that made it to the edge of the swarm now faced an aerial attack. I watched one of the birds: the bi-coloured ant bird has two middle toes fused at the base, and minute projections on the soles of its feet. These two tools help it to gain a powerful grip on twigs, even if they're slippery from rain. I watched the bird confidently rotate round on its perch, until it spotted a small cockroach. It relaxed its grip and used its powerful leg muscles to launch away from the twig to land on the prey. Other ant birds, there were about six in attendance, used similar techniques of sitting, watching, then pouncing. Small creatures were being snaffled up all around me.

One column of ants had ascended a tree. They were in a two-way stream: those going up were empty jawed, while those coming down had their mouths full of wriggling succulent termite grubs. I could just see the shape of the clay termite nest that they were raiding some twenty metres up. Now the sub-majors in the ant legions around my feet came into their own. Busily they transported prey, body parts or, if they were small enough to carry, complete carcasses back to the queen and the main colony. If a grasshopper leg was too large for a single worker, two co-operated to carry the burden. Up to 100,000 prey items can be killed and eaten each day, not including the by-catch that goes to the birds. These raids are so devastating, that they can clear an entire area. So each day the hunting party sets out in a different direction to give each 'killing field' time to recover. Army ant colonies usually need about a square kilometre of rainforest to sustain their rapacious appetites. I followed the columns back to my tent and the giant tree. They scampered over the outside of my tent. I'd have to wait until they were all back before I could take it down.

Now I wanted to see what was inside that hole in the buttress root. Treading carefully to avoid any ants, I crouched down and shone my torch upwards. My breath was taken away by the amazing sight. The bivouac or encampment was made entirely of the ants themselves. By hooking the claws of their legs together, they made a wall of interlaced insects. The queen and the young were protected by the wall. All those bodies also kept them warm. The interior of the bivouac is four times as warm as the outside temperature. Sometimes the ants camp right out in the open, but wherever they are, these camps are temporary.

Because of the huge amounts of food that they need, army ants are nomadic. So the colony never stays in one place for long. In some periods they move more often. The ant colony lives in a cycle which goes between two phases of activity, each of which lasts about twenty days. The colony I'd camped next to hadn't moved from this bivouac site for between forty-eight and seventy-two hours, so it was in the phase known as the stationary phase. That's when the queen needs to stay put to develop and then lay a new cluster of 100,000 to 300,000 eggs. The nomadic phase begins when these eggs hatch and the young larvae need a lot of food to grow. Then the colony will emigrate to a new bivouac site every night, so each day the raiding party is in a totally new hunting territory.

The queen doesn't lay any eggs in this phase,

but once the new batch of larvae is about ready to transform into new workers, the colony will fix up a new bivouac site once again.

One day I would like to see a bivouac on the move. The workers gently straddle the grubs, stretching their legs over their fat bodies, so they can run, holding their precious cargo beneath them. Towards the end of the move there is a royal procession. Most of the time it's impossible to see the queen because she's shielded by so many soldiers. Occasionally you may get a glimpse when somebody makes a mistake and the queen goes one way and her bodyguards go the other, but only for a split second, until her protectors return to surround her. If this happens you can see, very briefly, the queen's bizarre sausage-shaped body.

The queen lives longer than worker ants and can make the ripe old age of four years. When a colony becomes really huge, it will split into two. A new queen will be produced and she'll leave with half of the workers to set up a new colony. This is also the only time that males play a part in army ant society, because flying males leave to find and mate with any virgin queens.

Ant societies are all incredible, but army ants are particularly astonishing. Working co-operatively, hundreds of thousands of individuals turn themselves into a ruthless predator – an individual, a super organism – made up of tiny components or even a small group of individuals which are relatively harmless. But half a million of these insects together are as formidable, perhaps even more so than a jaguar or tiger. My close-up look at a swarm raid of army ants certainly made a huge impression on me.

This ant colony at work, one of nature's greatest dramas of life and death, is played out thousands of times every day in the New World Tropics. But as with so many rainforest phenomena, every year there are fewer places to see it. Army ants and their gaudy entourage of ant-following birds disappear when the forests are cut down. The forests are replaced by towns or cocoa plantations with banana trees for shade, but these new habitats just don't cut the mustard for creatures that have evolved for millennia in dense jungle. Forest destruction is happening at a terrifying rate. The future of remarkable spectacles of the natural world such as I had witnessed when I looked down at the floor blackened with scurrying ants and heard the excited cries of ant birds as they plunge and dive for any creatures fleeing the swarm, is in our hands. It is up to us to save these forests before it is too late.

Ant – Fact Box

● African driver ant colonies can have twenty million individuals and weigh up to twenty kilograms.

● The jaws of army ant soldiers are so powerful they can be used as stitches for cuts. The ant bites across the wound, the body is then pulled off, leaving the jaws and head attached.

● Ants are champion weightlifters and can carry objects ten times their body weight.

● If a swarm of African driver ants come across a tethered cow or horse, they can kill it, tearing apart its flesh to take back to feed the queen and her brood.

● Almost all ants in the world are females, including worker ants. Ant societies are a sisterhood – males are only produced when there are new queens about to start a new colony.

Science with the squishy bits left in!

Also available:

Ugly Bugs
The insect world goes under the magnifying glass.
Observe some foul families of bugs, discover the
secrets of strange scientists and test the theories
of insect disguise. It's swarming with info!

Blood, Bones and Body Bits
This book will get right under your skin! Test the
theories of your own brain power, discover the
secrets of strange scientists and learn how to
diagnose deadly diseases.

Nasty Nature
Have a whale of a time finding out about the
animal world! Grapple with some very ferocious
creatures, meet some nosey naturalists and learn
how to get on with a gorilla. You'll be howling
for more!

Chemical Chaos

Put chaotic chemistry to the test! Uncover the facts about experiments that went horribly wrong, discover the secrets of strange scientists and try your hand at quirky chemistry in your own kitchen.

Fatal Forces

Can you resist the urge to discover why your ears stop you falling off your bike? You'll also find out what keeps the moon in the sky, how quickly your fingernails grow ... and what happens when an apple smacks a scientist on the bonce!

Sounds Dreadful

Lift the lid on noise and find out how sound waves make your ear drums tremble, how a microphone turns your voice into electrical pulses ... and why you might get a nose bleed listening to church bells. It's a real scream!

Evolve or Die

Why are we still here when other creatures have been turned to stone, for ever? Go back millions of years to see insects as big as birds, fish with teeth and why chimps could be related to you.

Vicious Veg

Get stuck into a feast of info. and discover which plants eat dead insects for breakfast, why stinging nettles grow on old skeletons and which fungi can make your toes drop off. It's bloomin' amazing!

Frightening Light

Discover what stops your eyeballs from falling out, why dead bodies can make ghostly glowing lights and how a laser beam can sizzle human flesh. It's blazing with info!

Suffering Scientists Special

Read the painful potted history of scientists and their discoveries, from the first Greek brainboxes to modern-day geniuses.

Deadly Diseases

From the common cold to shocking smallpox, find out what happens when your body comes under attack from germs. You'll meet some seriously dangerous diseases.

Look out for:

The Awfully Big Quiz Book
Do you have what it takes to challenge a chemist
or fool a physicist? The Awfully Big Quiz Book is
packed with hundreds of astounding science
questions for testing your friends, your teachers ...
and yourself.

Microscopic Monsters
Find out how toilet germs helped catch a thief,
which creature lays eggs between your toes, why
your toothbrush is covered in germs and what
makes your guts the perfect home for bacteria.
This is the tiny world of Science!

Explosive Experiments Special
A collection of experiments that will blow your
mind! Find out how famous scientists made some
of their most important discoveries and how you
can test a few theories at home!

Science has never been so horrible!

Geography with the gritty bits left in!

Have you seen:

Odious Oceans
Read our roving reporter's guide to the seabed,
uncover the dreadful details of the Titanic's last day
and see if you're nautical enough to join the Navy.

Violent Volcanoes
Find out about volcano survivors, get clued-up with
the spotter's guide to eruptions and plan an
explosive holiday with our very own volcano
vacation guide.

Raging Rivers
Join our heroic hydrologists on a turbulent river tour
from ice cap to ocean, read the secret diary of a
brave river explorer and get to know your watery
wildlife with our spotter's guide.

Desperate Deserts
Visit the desert where it snows, find out how to
make a tasty pudding from camel milk and why
cactus juice could be a deadly drink. Have you got
what it takes to survive?

Look out for:

Earth-shattering Earthquakes
With Syd the seismologist as your guide, take a tour round some of the world's most dangerous places as we see what it takes to make the earth shake, and what you should do if you're caught in an earthquake.

Freaky Peaks
Follow the adventures of mountain explorers, as they climb some of the world's highest mountains. You'll see the animals that live there, the plants that survive up mountains ... and whether or not the yeti really exists.